MW01089573

Who Hid It?

BY TARO GOMI

THE MILLBROOK PRESS · BROOKFIELD, CONNECTICUT

Who hid the glove?

Who hid the toothbrush?

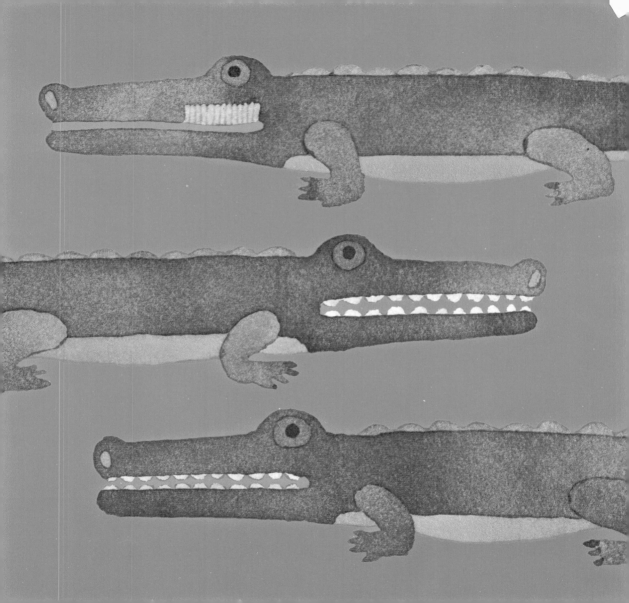

Who hid the sock?

Who hid the candles?

Who hid the cap?

Who hid the magnet?

Who hid the scooter?

Who hid the flag?

Who hid the pencils?

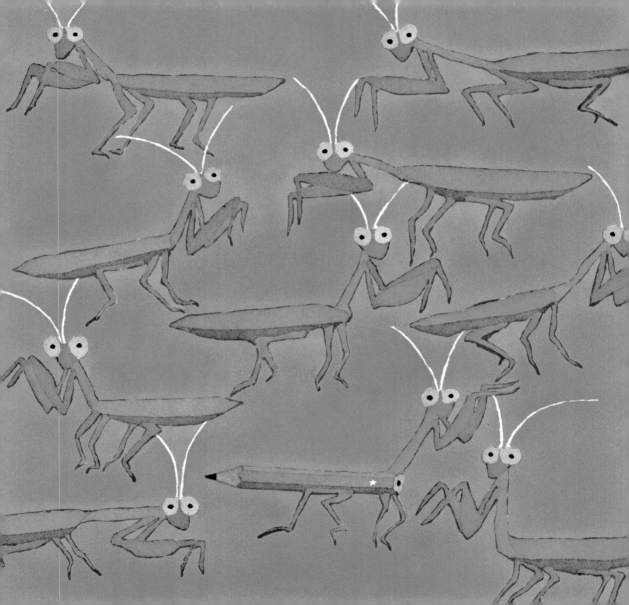

Who hid the cards?

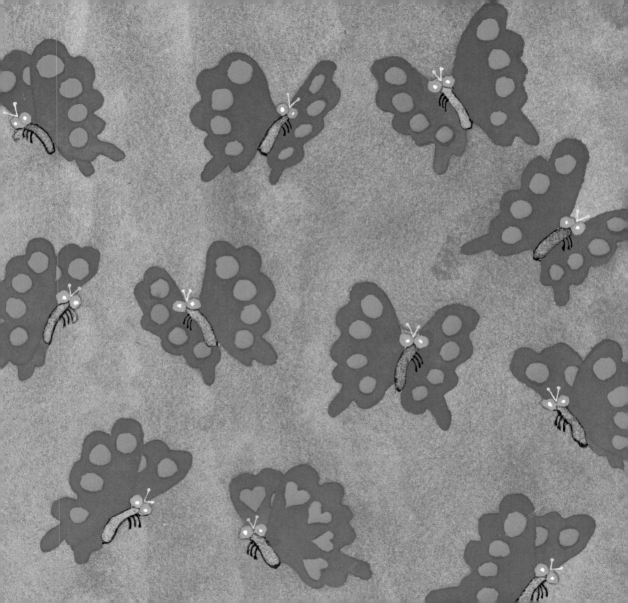

Who hid the fork and spoon?

Taro Gomi is an industrial and graphic designer as well as an author and illustrator of children's books. He writes in Japanese, but his books have been translated and sold all over the world.

This book and its companion volume *Who Ate It?* were Mr. Gomi's first works. They were awarded the Sankei Children's Publishing Culture Award in Japan and are in their forty-first printing there.

Children of all countries respond to the droll sense of humor that comes through in Mr. Gomi's art. His background as an industrial designer has also added to the appeal of his books. He is known for the careful thought he gives to every detail of his work and its manufacture—including the color reproduction, quality of paper, and even the size of the children's hands that will be holding his books.

Cataloging-in-Publication Data
Gomi, Taro.
Who hid it? / by Taro Gomi.
p. cm.-
Summary: Colorful illustrations display a familiar object and the simple text asks: "Who hid the . . . ?" It is answered by looking at the page on the right with its whole picture in which the object has been camouflaged.
ISBN 1-56294-011-2 (LIB.)   ISBN 1-56294-707-9 (TR.)
1. Visual perception.   2. Size and shape.   3. Color.
4. Easy reading materials.   I. Title.
1991
152.14 (E)

KAKUSHITANO DĀRE by Taro Gomi
Copyright © 1977 by Taro Gomi
(English translation rights arranged with Bunka Publishing Bureau through Japan Foreign-Rights Centre)